Glass Engraving

Sonia Lucano

Glass Engraving
25 Projects for the Home

Photographs by Frédéric Lucano

Design by Vania Leroy

POTTER
CRAFT

New York

Contents

A vase for every day of the week
/ templates page 43

Wine glasses
/ templates pages 44–45

Experiment with the size of the letters and different fonts when composing the names.

Star plates
/ templates page 43

Jungle glasses
/ templates pages 44–45

Plum bowl
/ template page 46

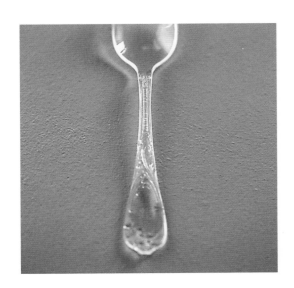

Water carafe
/ template pages 46–47

Jars
/ template page 47

Bottle on a bottle
/ templates page 48

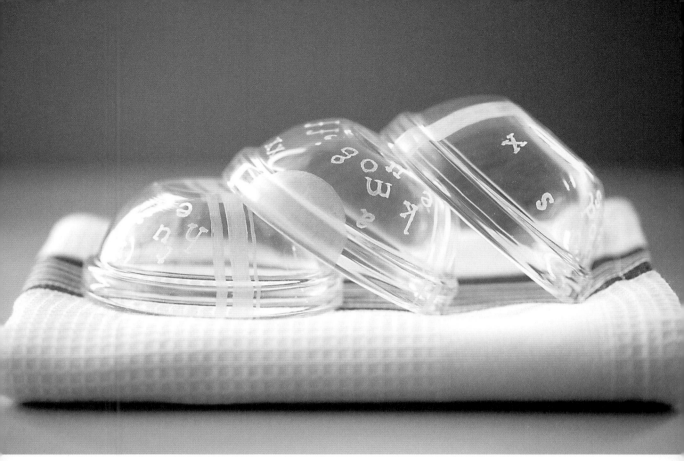

Small bowls
/ templates page 49

Photo frame
/ templates page 48

Personalize your photograph frame by engraving a name or a
message using the alphabet on page 48.
The engraving tool can also be used to highlight particular details
of the framed photograph.

Message stones
/ templates page 50

As a change from glass, try engraving stone. It is generally a much softer material than glass and is therefore easier to engrave. Follow the same procedure as for glass (page 39)—make sure the surface is clean and free from dust, draw your design on the stone with an indelible marker, and then engrave it as normal.

Stag vase
/ template page 50

Monogrammed glasses
/ templates page 51

Have fun intertwining letters to create glasses
personalized with your guests' initials.

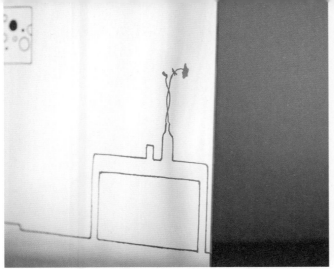

Light bulb
/ template page 53

Mirror
/ template pages 52–53

Colored glasses
/ templates page 54

Lamp no.5
/ templates page 54

Kids' plates

/ templates page 55

Preserving jar
/ template page 55

Silhouette pendant shade
/ templates page 56

Bubble lamp
/ templates page 57

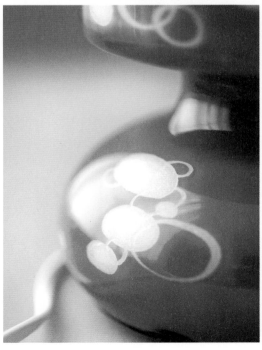

Pigeon candle holders
/ templates page 59

Candlestick vase
/ template page 58

Shot glasses
/ templates page 59

Apple pie dish
/ template pages 60–61

Equipment

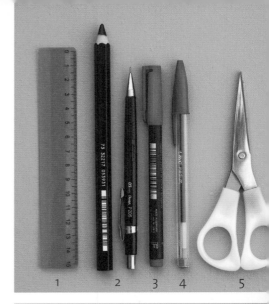

1 Ruler
2 Pencils
3 Indelible marker
4 Ballpoint pen
5 Scissors

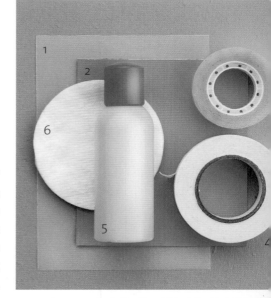

1 Engraving tool
2 Diamond
   grindstone and
   corundum grind
   wheels of different
   sizes and thicknesses
   are optional.

1 Tracing paper
2 Graphite paper (wax-free
   transfer paper)
3 Adhesive tape
4 Masking tape
5 Alcohol-based solvent
6 Clean cotton pad

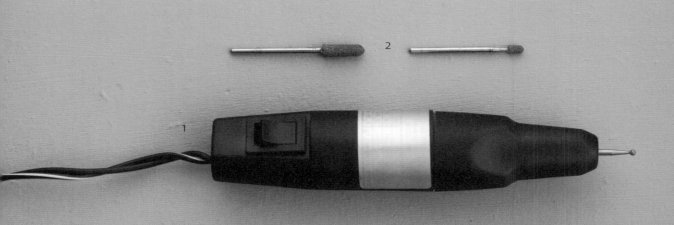

How to Engrave

The engraving tool is very easy to use, rather like a pencil. Practice first on an old glass jar or bottle. Always wash the glass before you start in order to remove any residual grease that would prevent the indelible marker from outlining the template clearly, or cause the engraving tool to slip.

Make sure your work area is comfortable and well lit: lay the item to be engraved on a cloth or a plain dark surface so that you can see the work clearly and support your hand at the same height as the item. When drawing the first lines, apply only very light pressure to avoid the tool skidding across the surface. You can apply slightly more pressure when drawing subsequent lines, as the engraving tool will follow in the path of the first line.

To avoid distortion, work so that you are looking down directly over the glass. Start by drawing the main outline and other principal lines of the design, working from the top downward and using a light continuous stroke to make a clean line.

There are many different kinds of glass:

Transparent glass
A wealth of glass objects can be used for engraving, including new items, recycled glass, and little treasures found in thrift stores. Hard glass is more difficult to engrave than soft glass, but the thicker the glass, the easier it is to work on.

Colored glass objects
If the glass is colored, the engraved designs will usually be fairly opaque. Some glass, however, is colored by adding a thin coat of paint to the surface. In this case, the engraving tool will not cut into the glass but merely remove the layer of paint, leaving a clear glass motif against a colored background. It is essential to work on the coated side with this type of glass.

Check carefully when choosing colored glass for engraving: Some glass appears colored, but is in fact merely coated in a colored film. This type of glass does not work well with the engraving tool.

Mirrors
Mirrors can be worked on in two ways. Engraving directly on the front of the mirror produces the classic opaque effect. Engraving on the back into the silvering—the reflective coating on the reverse of a mirror—produces a transparent effect.

Transferring a pattern to the inside of a glass object

1.
Use this method when it's possible to place the template inside the glass object. Trace the design onto tracing paper or make a photocopy of it to the size indicated.

2.
Cut around the design and place it inside the glass object. Use adhesive tape to hold the design in place.

3.
Trace the outline of the design on the outside of the glass with an indelible marker.

4.
Remove the tracing paper and carefully engrave the design. Blow regularly on the glass as you work to remove the dust left by the engraving tool.

5.
Using solvent and a clean cotton pad, remove any traces of the indelible marker.

1.
Use this method when the template cannot be fixed to the inside of the object.
Trace the design onto tracing paper or make a photocopy of it to the size indicated.

2.
Lay the pattern on a sheet of graphite paper (wax-free transfer paper).

3.
Use adhesive tape to hold both the template and the graphite paper to the glass. Make sure that the graphite side of the paper is face down on the glass. Trace the template with a ballpoint pen, pressing quite hard so that the design is transferred onto the glass.

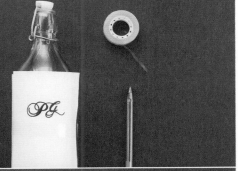

4.
Remove the graphite paper and template very carefully, being careful not to smudge the design left on the glass.

5.
Begin engraving, blowing regularly onto the glass as you work to remove the dust left by the engraving tool.

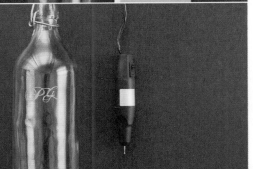

Making a pattern of dots

1.
Using a ruler, make pencil marks at ³⁄₄" (2cm) intervals on a piece of ³⁄₄" (2cm) wide masking tape (or use ³⁄₈" (1cm) wide tape and mark at ³⁄₈" (1cm) intervals).

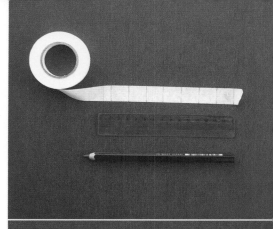

2.
Stick the tape onto the glass, then place another piece across it at a right angle, using the marks as a guide. Continue in this way until the glass is covered with a checked pattern. Mark a small dot at all the places where the pieces of tape cross with an indelible marker.

3.
Remove the tape and carefully engrave the dots. Blow regularly on the glass as you work to remove the dust left by the engraving tool.

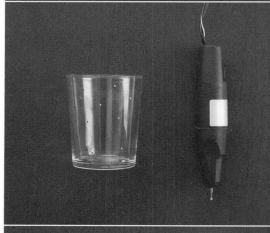

4.
Using solvent and a clean cotton pad, remove any remaining traces of the indelible marker.

1.
Trace the pattern onto tracing paper, or make a photocopy of it to the size indicated. Use one of the methods on pages 38 and 39 to transfer the design.

2.
Engrave the outline of the design with the diamond grindstone.

3.
Shade the required areas of the design using a corundum grind wheel. It grinds more of the surface than the diamond grindstone. If your engraving tool only has a diamond tip, press down lightly and use stippling to cover the design.

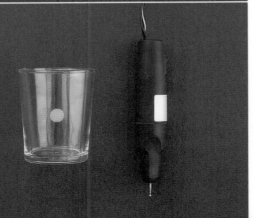

4.
You may need to go over the design again with the diamond grindstone to ensure that the shading is even.

The templates

Begin by tracing the templates onto tracing paper or making a photocopy of them to the size indicated, then follow the instructions given on pages 37–41. Remember you can always adapt the size of the template to suit the object you want to engrave by enlarging or reducing it using a photocopier.

A vase for every day of the week
/ pages 6–7

Increase size of templates to 200%

1234567890

Star plates
/ page 8

Increase size of templates to 200%

ABCDEFGHIJKLMNOPQRSTU

abcdefghijklmnopqrstuvwxyz

abcdefghijklmnopqrstuvwxyz

abcdefghijklmnopqrstuvwxyz ABCDEFGHIJKL

abcdefghijklmnopqrstuvwxyz

honoRé   MadEleiNe

VWXYZ abcdefghijklmnopqrstuvwxyz

ABCDEFGHIJKLMNOPQRSTUVWXYZ

abcdefghijklmnopqrstuvwxyz

MNOPQRSTUVWXYZ

Jungle glasses
/ pages 10–11

Templates are reproduced actual size

Water carafe
/ page 12
Template is reproduced actual size

Plum bowl
/ page 13
Increase size of template to 150%

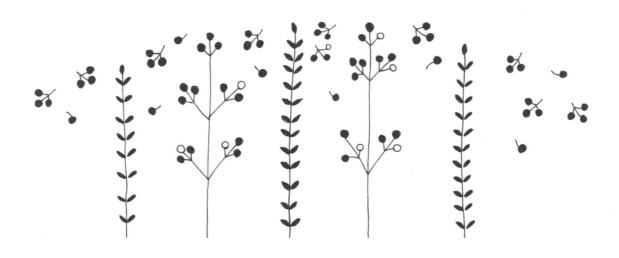

Jars

/ page 14

Template is reproduced actual size

Bottle on a bottle

/ page 15

Templates are reproduced actual size

Photo frame

/ page 16

Templates are reproduced actual size

0 1 2 3 4 5 6 7 8 9

(a b c d e f g h i j k l m n o p q r s t u v w x y z)

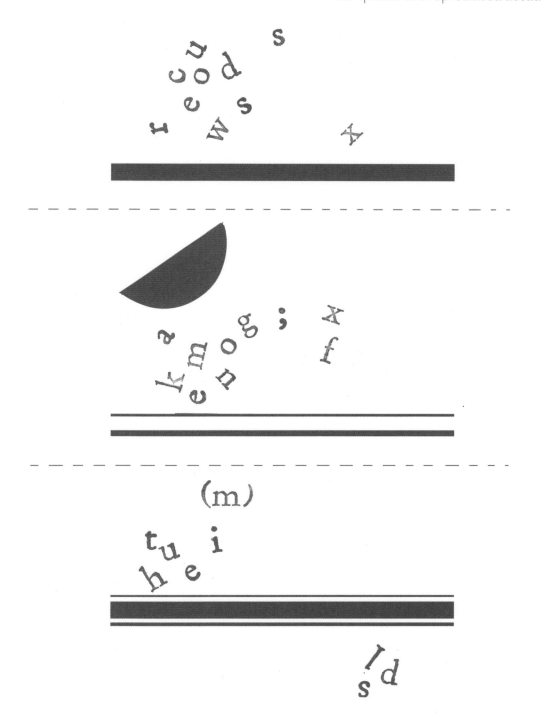

Stag vase
/ page 18
Template is reproduced actual size

. . .

Message stones
/ page 19
Templates are reproduced actual size

white.

100 % recycle

13

LovE

Monogrammed glasses

/ pages 20–21

Templates are reproduced actual size

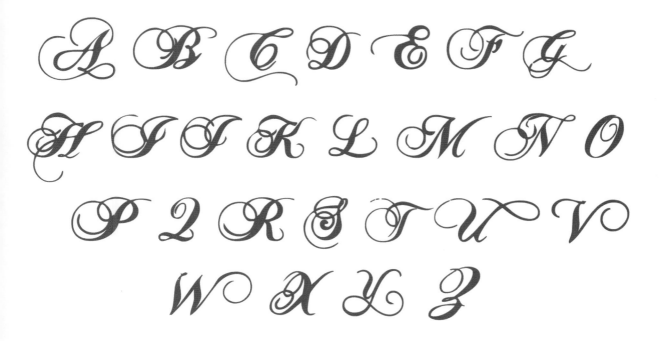

Mirror

/ page 22

Template is reproduced actual size

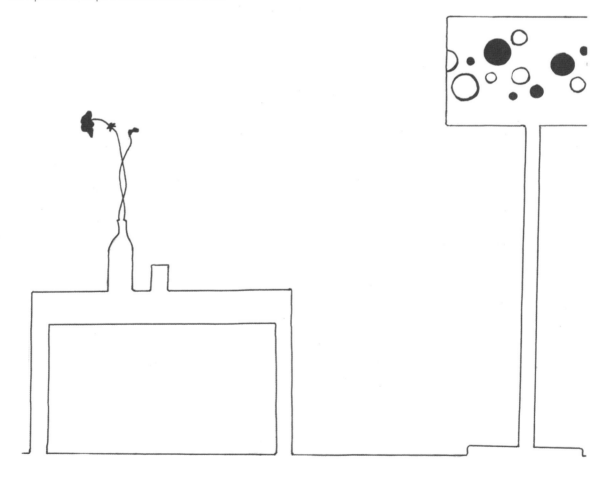

Light bulb
/ page 23
Template is reproduced actual size

Lamp no.5
/ page 24

Templates are reproduced actual size

Colored glasses
/ page 25

Templates are reproduced actual size

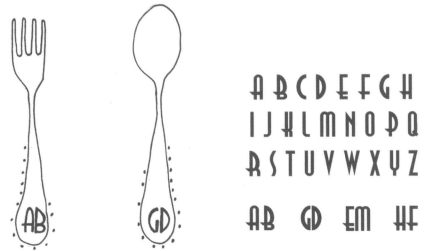

Kids' plates
/ pages 26-27
Templates are reproduced actual size

A B C D E F G H I J K L
M N O P Q R S T U V
W X Y Z

BATMAN IS MY HERO

WONDER WOMAN TOO

Preserving jar
/ page 28
Template is reproduced actual size (or follow the instructions on page 40 to make the dots)

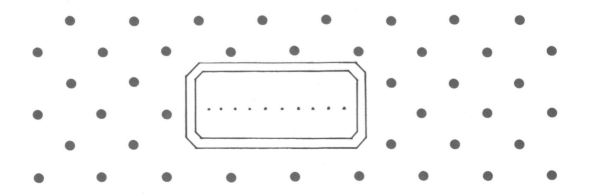

Silhouette pendant shade

/ page 29

Templates are reproduced actual size

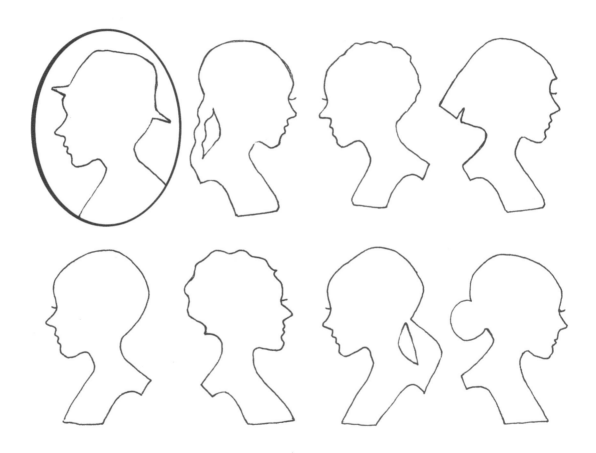

Bubble lamp
/ pages 30–31
Templates are reproduced actual size

Candlestick vase
/ page 32

Template is reproduced actual size

Pigeon candle holders

/ page 33

Templates are reproduced actual size

Shot glasses

/ page 34

Templates are reproduced actual size

1. Hieracifella   2. Tenaetum   3. Petasites

Apple pie dish

/ page 35

Template is reproduced actual size

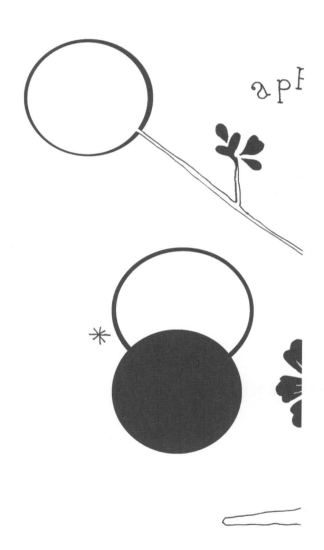

ple pie.

*

(13)

Resources

Inexpensive glass engraving tools, such as the Inscriblio Engraving Tool by EK Success, the Amaco Diamond-Tipped Glass Engraver, and the Inland EasyMark Electric Engraver, can be found at local craft stores and at big chain craft stores. They can also be ordered directly from the manufacturer. A Dremel tool can be used to engrave glass, though the cost of a Dremel is generally about three times that of an engraving tool. Dremel brand tools can be found at local hardware stores as well as chain home improvement stores. Always read the manufacturer's instructions carefully before using any tool.

Engraving Tools

A.C. Moore
Arts & Crafts
866-342-8802
www.acmoore.com

Amaco
800-374-1600
www.amaco.com

Dick Blick
Art Materials
800-828-4548
www.dickblick.com

EK Success
800-524-1349
www.eksuccess.com

Inland
800-521-8428
www.inlandlapidary.com

Jo-Ann
Fabric and Craft Stores
888-739-4120
www.joann.com

Michaels
Arts, Crafts & More
800-642-4235
www.michaels.com

Dremel Rotary Tool

Lowe's Home Improvement
800-445-6937
www.lowes.com

Home Depot
800-553-3199
www.homedepot.com

Target Corporation
800-440-0680
www.target.com

Index

Acknowledgments

A very big thank you to Fred, also to Pascale Kogan, Vania Leroy, Muriel Tepic and Dominique Montembault, and to Marabout for producing this book which is so dear to my heart.

Translation copyright © 2009 by Marabout

Published in the United States by Potter Craft, an imprint of the Crown Publishing Group, a division of Random House, Inc., New York.
www.crownpublishing.com
www.pottercraft.com

POTTER CRAFT and colophon is a registered trademark of Random House, Inc.

Originally published in France as Verre gravé by Marabout (Hachette Livre), Paris, in 2008.
Copyright © 2008 by Marabout.

Library of Congress Cataloging-in-Publication Data is available upon request.

ISBN: 978-0-307-45237-5

Printed in China

1 3 5 7 9 10 8 6 4 2

First American Edition